I Declare War: Spiritual Warfare Declarations

Photo Credit: Preston Knowles Photography

I DECLARE WAR: SPIRITUAL WARFARE DECLARATIONS

DR. TAVARA JOHNSON

I Declare War: Spiritual Warfare Declarations

DEDICATION

This book is dedicated to those who have lost
hope in the promises of God because of their
wait or process. It's time for you to possess what
has been predestined to you from the foundation
of the world. I pray these declarations give you
hope and inspire you to get back in the fight
again and declare war!

FOREWORD
By Jekalyn Carr
Author, "You Will Win"

From the first time I met Dr. Tavara Johnson I knew she was one of God's choice vessels. She had all the qualities of an anointed scribe with a strategic message to the masses. She embodies the Christlike image with class, charisma, and most importantly, genuineness. Today, I write this foreword to her captivating book, "I Declare War" because I believe it is a powerful tool for serious and sustained spiritual development as we focus on the core principles that belongs in the war room of all believers.

Reading this book, you will find it hard to defend the view that good warriors are born, not made. Dr. Johnson provides compelling scriptural & practical evidence that all believers should practice with serious and sustained effort. What better way to strengthen the quality of decreeing and declaring as we should? I hope that this book will become a primer for Apostles, Prophets, Evangelist, Pastors and Teachers, helping warriors across the country to learn and practice the art of Spiritual Warfare against the enemy.

TABLE OF CONTENTS

INTRODUCTION

Declarations allow you to make an announcement to the spiritual realm and express your faith in God. The bible declares to us that without faith it is impossible to please God and if you come to Him you must believe that He is a rewarder of those who diligently seek Him (Hebrews 11:16). If you are not declaring the word of God over your life and circumstances, there is no activation to the promises of God. Declarations can be used to change the trajectory of our lives for the better. The bible declares in Job 22:28 "when you decree a thing it shall be established," and therefore it is vital to speak what you desire to see or have according to the will of God for your life.

There is power in your words and you must know the weight that it carries. The first revelation of the power of words was found in Genesis 1:3 which declares God said, "let there be light and there was light". Again, this speaks to the energy words carry in the universe. Words spoken (whether negative or positive) are constantly circling in the atmosphere waiting for time and chance to collide. The bible declares that life and death are in the power of the tongue and those who love it will eat the fruit (Proverbs

1

18:21). We determine the outcome based on what we decide to verbalize or not to verbalize. Also, it is important to note the spiritual realm cannot discern whether you are being facetious or not with your speech, so make a conscientious effort to monitor the words you speak.

Declarations located in this book are based on scripture and the word of God. Declarations based on the promises of God and the will of God causes Heaven to respond. The bible declares God is not a man that He shall lie so if He said it, it shall come to pass. There is assurance in knowing that God is always watching over His word (spoken) to perform it. The vigilance God displays over His word indicates His love and desire for us to experience the manifestation and the abundant life that was predestined for us.

Declarations are like prayers and these are ways in which you can communicate with your Heavenly Father. As you say these declarations, do so with the power and authority given to you by God. You are a part of a chosen generation so know that you have the victory and receive it by faith.

Remember, it is imperative that you remain in good standing with God. Get in the habit of repenting daily and asking for forgiveness before making your petition (declarations) to ensure the courts of Heaven will respond favorably to your request.

DAILY CONFESSIONS

I decree and declare I can discern my time and seasons like the sons of Issachar. ~**1 Chronicles 12:32**

I decree and declare the Lord will help me to recognize my destiny helpers sent to run with the vision. ~**Habakkuk 2:2**

Lord I believe that you know the plans for me, and it is to bless me with a great future. ~**Jeremiah 29:11**

I decree and declare every curse of infirmity, sickness and premature death is broken in Jesus name.

I trust the Lord to lead me and guide my footsteps so they will not slide. I will not lean to my own understanding but acknowledge God in all my ways to ensure that I make the right decisions based on his instructions. ~**Proverbs 3:5-6**

Lord, I know you are near to me because I love you and call on you. ~**Psalm 145:18**

Lord, plead my cause against them that strive with me and fight against them that fight against me. **~Psalm 35: 1-2**

Lord, you said when a man's ways pleases you, even their enemies will be at peace with them. I decree and declare peace is my portion. **~Proverbs 16:7**

Lord, download multi-millionaire ideas and inventions into my spirit. **~Proverbs 8:12**

It is written that I don't wrestle against flesh and blood but against principalities, powers, rulers and wickedness in high place. **~Ephesians 6:12**

Lord, every mandate, order or sanction sent to curse my prosperity, may it be consumed by the fire of God.

Lord, because I seek the kingdom of God and its righteousness all things will be added unto me.

I take the sword of the Lord and apply it to the root and cut off all spirits attached to anti-progress in my life.

I break every spirit of limitation off my life preventing me from obtaining wealth.

I sever every illegal and demonic soul tie that will give the enemy access to my mind.

I plead the power of the blood of Jesus Christ all over my mind.

I curse every generational curse in my lineage trying to pass on to my children. The line has been drawn in the sand and they are off limits.

I seal these declarations in the name of Jesus!
Amen

DECLARATIONS FOR VISION

2 Corinthians 5:7 declares "For we walk by faith, not by sight". But the truth is, if you don't have vision or foresight into what is to come or what God desires to do in your life it will be difficult for you to have faith in God because you cannot see. Walking by faith requires you to see through the spiritual lens of God and not through the tangible world you live in. Hebrews 11:6 declares "But without faith it is impossible to please Him, for he who comes to God must believe that He is, and that He is a rewarder of those who diligently seek Him."

Do you believe that you can attain what you are seeking God for? God is not a man that He shall lie. Trust that your seeking is not in vain. There are so many facets of God to know even though we will never know it all, but you can trust Him even when you can't trace Him. Spending time in the presence of God is important because He gives you revelation to know what is coming (whether positive or negative). Also, you will know how to strategize especially when it comes to negative circumstances even though you may not know the severity or the extent of the impact. He will give you specific instructions on how to obtain victory. A part of the reward in seeking God is the ability to gain beforehand knowledge or revelation.

- I decree and declare that I have 20/20 vision.
- I decree and declare my vision is like the eagle and I can see from a great distance.
- I decree and declare that the Lord will enlighten the eyes of my understanding.
- I decree and declare the Lord will increase my prayer life because prayer is where I will obtain strategies, witty ideas and inventions from God to create wealth.
- I decree and declare the Lord will give me the endurance to work every vision He has given to me. I will not back up or allow the spirit of fear or sabotage to cause me not to allow God to do what He wants to do in my life.
- Lord, I decree and declare that you will help me to see how to maximize the little that I have because plenty is in it when You are in it.
- I decree and declare that eyes have not seen, nor ears have heard the things God is getting ready to do in my life. ~1 **Corinthians 2:9**

- Lord, I decree and declare that I can discern the spirit of laziness and slothfulness and stop it in its track.
- Lord, I decree and declare that I will see success, increase and manifestation this year.
- I decree and declare that God is removing scales from both my spiritual and natural eyes. **~Psalm 119:18**
- I decree and declare that God is revealing and illuminating every secret and hidden thing. **~Luke 8:17**
- I decree and declare that I will never lose sight of God and who He is.
- I decree and declare God will open my eyes to see the plans that He has for me. **~Jeremiah 29:11**
- Lord, I decree and declare that you are enlarging my vision and my territory. **~1 Chronicles 4:20**
- I decree and declare that God is giving me the gift of knowledge and revelation.
- I decree and declare my ability to see will cause me to be favored on every level.
- Lord, I decree and declare you will give me the ability to see anything that is a hindrance and give me the strength to conquer it.

I seal these declarations in the name of Jesus!
Amen

DECLARATIONS FOR HEALING

Healing is the children's bread and it is available to all by God's finished work on the cross. Healing is something that is chosen daily. Why? Our lifestyles and what we intake daily confirm this. The type of foods that we consume as well as the toxicity allowed in our lives determine whether we will experience healing. For many, there are diseases passed on from one generation to another for various reasons. In some instances, unforgiveness plays a role, and because some family members are inflicted with certain ailments, it does not mean that it must be your portion.

Hence, the importance of you opening your mouth and making a bold declaration against it. 1 Peter 5:7 admonishes you to cast your cares on God because He cares for you. Simply put, do not hold onto issues or matters of the heart any longer than needed to prevent unwanted sickness. Additionally, there are many that have unforgiveness in their hearts and this can be a hindrance to prayers as well as lead people to experiencing sickness within their bodies.

- I decree and declare that I am forgiven from any door that I may have opened knowingly or unknowingly that allowed any sickness and disease to come in.
- I decree Jehovah Rapha is my healer.
- I decree and declare I will live and not die. **~Psalm 118:17**
- I decree and declare all reproductive issues in my body will wither up and die.
- I decree and declare all pain will leave my body now.
- I decree and declare God is healing my broken heart and is near to me. **~Psalm 34:18**
- I decree and declare all spirits of infirmity that came in by way of witchcraft is cast out.
- I decree and declare I will walk in good health even as my soul prospers. **~3 John 2**
- I decree and declare all sickness and disease that came in through my bloodline is broken and dismantled.
- I decree and declare my body will line up based on the word of God for my life. **~Psalm 139:14**
- I decree and declare all spirits of infirmity that came in by way of trauma and accidents are cast out.

- I decree and declare I will not fear or be dismayed because the Lord is with me. **~Isaiah 41:10**
- I decree and declare no sickness, disease or plague shall come nigh my dwelling. **~Psalm 91:10**
- I decree and declare that I am redeemed by the blood of Jesus and no sickness or disease can harm me. **~1 Peter 1:18-20**
- I decree and declare Jesus was wounded for my transgressions, He was bruised for my iniquities and by His stripes I am healed. **~Isaiah 53:5**
- I speak to all cancer cells and command you to wither up and die.
- I decree and declare all spirits of hypertension, low blood, diabetes, thyroids and blood diseases are stripped from their powers.
- I decree and declare I will take the shield of faith and quench every fiery dart of the enemy. **~Ephesians 6:16**
- I decree and declare that my health and body is released from all diabolical assignments from the enemy.

I seal these declarations in the name of Jesus! Amen

DECLARATIONS FOR SINGLES

Psalm 37:4 says delight yourself in the Lord, and He will give you the desires of your heart. God knows your exact location and He has the perfect timing for the manifestation of His promises in your life. I admonish you to be wise about your season of singleness and embrace it. Don't just survive it but thrive in it. Spend time with God discovering your purpose and everything predestined for you so you can begin to walk in the fullness of it. Who better to get the master plan from than the one who has the blueprint for your life? Singles be mindful not to despise your single season but embrace it and allow God to do the work that He wants to do in you. Apostle Paul states that those who are single are free to do the work of the Lord without restrictions, versus someone who may be married.

Singles, if you are desiring marriage, trust that God will bring it to pass. Maximize your season of singleness to prevent carrying excess or unnecessary baggage into your season of marriage. Allow God to prepare you during your season of singleness like he did with Esther and

Ruth. For many of you, there are unhealthy soul ties that need to be broken and healing needed before you meet your God ordained mate. The bible declares in Genesis 2:18 that it is not good for man to be alone and that a suitable helper will be made for him. Simply put, you are someone's helpmate and your land is no longer barren but married (Isaiah 62:4).

- I decree and declare that the Lord strengthens me with all His might according to his glorious power and because of this I receive patience and longsuffering. ~**Colossians 1:11**
- I decree and declare that every word that proceeds out of the mouth of God concerning my life will not return unto him void, but it will accomplish everything that He said it would. ~**Isaiah 55:11**
- I decree and declare I will not be anxious for anything, but instead I will submit everything to God through prayer and supplication. I will give thanks knowing that He will hear my petition and provide me with the peace that surpasses all human understanding that will guard my heart and mind. ~**Philippians 4:6-7**
- I decree and declare the fire of God will consume all incubus and succubus spirits.

- I decree and declare that the Lord has commanded the blessings upon me and my storehouses and everything I put my hands to shall prosper. **~Deuteronomy 28:8**
- I decree and declare that I am healed and whole and because of it I have the ability to recognize my purpose partner. ~ **Proverbs 18:22**
- I decree and declare that the sword of the Lord severs all illegal and unhealthy soul ties blocking my marriage in the name of Jesus.
- I decree and declare all demonic marriage certificates, wedding dresses and rings that was buried to prevent me from being married be dug up and consume by the fire of the Holy Ghost.
- I decree and declare every power behind a cycle of broken relationships be destroyed by the thunder of God. **~Ephesians 6:12**
- I decree and declare all counterfeit spirits sent from the enemy will be arrested today.
- I decree and declare that the joy of the Lord will always be my strength. **~Nehemiah 8:10**
- I decree and declare in God's perfect timing He will release my husband that

would make me rich and add no sorrow. **~Proverbs 10:22**
- I decree and declare the Lord will deliver me from every trap and snare of the enemy and give me victory over every temptation that I may not sin against you or myself. **~1 Corinthians 6 18-20**
- Father, I believe in your word and declare that my status has changed. I am no longer called forsaken or desolate, but I shall be called married and you will delight in me. **~Isaiah 62:4**
- I decree and declare any spiritual husband repelling my God ordained spouse be stripped of their powers and tied with chains.

I seal these declarations in the name of Jesus!
Amen

DECLARATIONS FOR MARRIAGES

The institution of marriage was created and ordained by God (Mark 10: 6-9). God initiated the first wedding ceremony in the book of Genesis with Adam and Eve. It is imperative that those who are married understand that marriage is ministry and it is designed to be a representation of God and His bride (church). Perceiving marriage through the eyes of God will dictate the way spouses treat one another. God has commanded us to be fruitful, multiply and have dominion over the earth. **(Genesis 1:28)** This tells me that godly marriages should be reigning and dominating all over the world. There is power in unity and this is why the institution of marriage is under attack. The bible asks the question, how can two walk together except they agree?

Husbands and wives must ensure they become one flesh by sharing the same goals, visions and belief system to carry out the mandate by God for their marriage. Husbands and wives, marriage is a lifelong commitment and an oath made to God in the company of witnesses. Be vigilant in your marriages and fight daily for your spouses because the enemy is always seeking a way to bring discord and division. Pray without ceasing about the success of your marriage. Ensure there is constant communication with God as humans do not have the ability to read minds and determine healthy alternatives for dealing with arguments. Always remember you have a duty to cover your God ordained marriage.

- I decree and declare that we are one in soul, mind, body and spirit.
- I decree and declare we are patient and kind with one another in our marriage. **~1 Corinthians 13:4-5**
- I decree and declare that we will grow deeper in love with each other and mutually help one another. **~Ecclesiastes 4:9**
- I decree and declare marriage is ministry and we will fulfill the purpose that God intended us to.
- I decree and declare that we will not let the sun go down on any disagreement we may have that could potentially bring division. **~Ephesians 4:26**
- I decree and declare divine favor over my marriage.

- I decree and declare that I am a wise woman and I choose to build my house and not tear it down. **~Proverbs 14:1**
- I decree and declare that we will love one another unconditionally.
- I decree and declare that we will be devoted to one another and will place each other above ourselves. **~Romans 12:10**
- I decree and declare that I am my husband's favor because he has found a good thing. **~Proverbs 18:22**
- I decree and declare that the spirit of Jezebel or Delilah will not be able to penetrate the bond of our marriage. ~ **Judges 16:19**
- I decree and declare that our marriage will be a beacon of light for those desiring marriage or in need of restoration in their marriage.
- I decree and declare that what God has joined together, no man will put asunder. **~Mark 10:9**
- I decree and declare that no weapon that forms against our marriage shall be able to prosper. **~Isaiah 54:17**
- I decree and declare that I am my husband's God ordained helper. **~Genesis 2:18**

- I decree and declare we are one flesh and nothing and no one can tear us apart. **~Matthew 19:4-6**
- I decree and declare that my noble character will bring honor to my husband and I will not be a disgrace to him. **~Proverbs 12:4**
- I decree and declare that we will continually give praise and thanks to God in every situation we may find ourselves in. **~1 Thessalonians. 5:17-18**
- I decree and declare we will not deprive one another, but we will devote ourselves to one another to prevent temptation in that area. **~1 Corinthians 7:5**
- I decree and declare God will supply all our needs according to his riches in glory in Christ Jesus. **~Philippians. 4:19**

I seal these declarations in the name of Jesus!

Amen

DECLARATIONS FOR CHILDREN

Children are a gift and blessing from God. There is a reason why God admonishes us to be like little children. Children are pure and their faith towards the promises of their parents do not waiver. This is one of the reasons God calls us to have childlike faith because He expects for us to respond in the same manner with Him (Matthew 18:2-4). It is crucial that children are always protected by any means necessary. The enemy has a way of attacking the children from an early age to corrupt their innocence and wound them to prevent them from walking into their God ordained destiny.

Children are a part of the next generation and we must push them in purpose from an early age and help them to hear the voice of God. When we look at 1Samuel 3, we see that Eli trained Samuel to hear the voice of the Lord. Samuel thought Eli was calling him, but Eli realized it was God trying to get his attention. Those caring for children have a duty to bring them up in the fear of the Lord and provide

proper training as they grow (Proverbs 22:6).
Also, leaving an inheritance for the children is
something that God requires of parents or those
responsible for children.

- I decree and declare my children will be
  the head and not the tail and they will be
  above only. ~**Deuteronomy 28:13**
- I decree and declare my children will
  stand out and excel above their peers in
  every area of their lives.
- I decree and declare godly wisdom and
  counsel will be their portion and they will
  be connected to godly people. ~**Psalm
  37:30**
- I decree and declare my children dwell in
  the secret place of the most High and no
  plague will come nigh their dwelling.
  ~**Psalm 91:1**
- I decree and declare my children will
  obtain full tuition and scholarships for
  schooling.
- I decree and declare favor and mercy will
  follow them all the days of their lives.
  ~**Psalm 23:6**
- I decree and declare they will keep their
  innocence until marriage.
- I decree and declare my unborn baby is
  healthy and no weapon formed against
  them shall prosper. ~**Isaiah 54:17**

- I decree and declare the Lord will watch over my children in their going and coming. ~**Psalm 121:8**
- I decree and declare you have called them to the nations, and you will show forth your glory through them. ~**Isaiah 55:5**
- I decree and declare that my children will know of your voice from an early age. ~**2 Timothy 3:15**
- I decree and declare that as I train up the children according to your laws and statutes, they will not depart from it as they grow older. ~**Proverbs 22:6**
- God, I decree and declare that you are regulating the minds of the children and they will not fall victim to peer pressure or suicide. ~**1Peter 5:7**
- Lord, I decree and declare you have great plans for my children. ~**Jeremiah 29:11**
- I decree and declare that my children will begin to develop their gifts from an early age.
- I decree and declare every invisible limitation and wall set by demonic agents is broken in the name of Jesus.
- I decree and declare my children will break records and barriers.
- I decree and declare my children have hinds' feet to walk on high places. ~**Habakkuk 3:19**

- I decree and declare that the Lord is increasing my children's discernment and spiritual vision.

I seal these declarations in the name of Jesus!
Amen

DECLARATIONS FOR FAMILY

The book of Genesis 4 depicts the first representation of a nuclear family with Adam and Eve and their two children Cain and Able. Today, the nuclear family as we know it is being attacked with some attempting to redefine it. Families are not perfect, but it is vital that persons make a conscience effort to protect it. Family is extremely sacred to God in that one of the commandments is for children to honor their mother and father so that they will experience long life. Children, this statement is clearly stating the need to respect your parents no matter the situation. God's plan is perfect, and He knew that you would be born into the family that you are a part of. Families that are estranged, know that the hour has come to mend broken relationships.

Time is of the essence and forgiveness is needed and required if we are expecting God to forgive us. Always remember that offering forgiveness to an individual is mainly for you and not for them. Holding onto unforgiveness essentially means that you are keeping the individual imprisoned in chains. Take a moment and I want you to use your imagination and perceive what that looks like. How does it make you feel? If you did not view unforgiveness in that manner and now you do, I want you to release the individual from the prison you were holding them in. I admonish you to forgive because God desires for us to live in love and unity.

- I decree and declare that our children, finances, and endeavors are blessed by God and will bring him glory and honor.
- I decree and declare God is supplying all my family needs according to His riches in glory. **~Philippians 4:19**
- I decree and declare that no weapon that forms against my family shall prosper. **~Isaiah 54:17**
- I decree and declare my house will be known as a house of prayer. **~Isaiah 56:7**
- I decree and declare that the fire of God is consuming all generational curses and spirits assigned to my family.
- I decree and declare that the joy of the Lord will be the strength of my family and anything trying to hinder our happiness will be destroyed. **~Psalm 28:7**
- I declare and decree that the voice of the enemy over my family life and household will be silenced and nullified.

- I decree and declare the blood of Jesus protects my family because we dwell in the secret place of the most high God. **~Psalm 91:1**
- I decree an declare the blessings of the Lord will make my family rich and add no sorrow. **~Proverbs 10:22**
- I decree and declare that as long as I train up a child in the way they should go, when they get older, they will not depart from it. **~Proverbs 22:6**
- I decree and declare total restoration and healing will be my family's portion.
- I decree and declare my family is blessed and anything they put their hands to shall be fruitful. **~Deuteronomy 12:7**
- I decree and declare that God's protective wall of fire covers me and my family. **~Zechariah 2:5**
- I decree and declare salvation will come to all my family members.
- I decree and declare only godly wisdom and counsel will be my family's portion. **~Proverbs 19:20**
- I decree and declare my family will walk into the fullness of what God has called them to be.
- I decree and declare that you are going before me and my family and making every crooked path straight. **~Isaiah 45:2**

- I decree and declare no spirit of jealousy and envy will be able to penetrate the hearts of my family members.
- I decree and declare that God is making every mountain low and every valley high in the lives of my family. **~Isaiah 40:4**
- I decree and declare that my family will rise and shine because the glory of the Lord has risen upon us. **~Isaiah 60:1**

I seal these declarations in the name of Jesus!
Amen

DECLARATIONS FOR PROMOTION

God desires to bless His children with an abundant life and inheritance. Promotion will not always signify material or natural advancement. However, through your seeking and quality time with God, many times you will receive spiritual promotion. When you are elevated spiritually, there are levels of dimensions that you have access to. You will place yourself in a position of authority to call those things into alignment that are not as though they are, and heaven will respond. God has given you power to decree your desires to be established. Whether you are expecting God to favor you naturally or spiritually, there is action that will need to be combined with your faith.

The bible declares to us that faith without works is dead (James 2:14). Often, people state that they are waiting on God when He is really waiting on them. At any moment God can catapult you into a season of promotion so stay in expectation. Expectation is the breeding ground for miracles to happen. Also, it is important that you obtain promotion the ethical and godly way. If you are required to compromise your integrity and values to attain it, then it is not from God. The bible clearly declares, the blessing of the Lord makes it rich and add no sorrow (Proverbs 10:22).

- I decree and declare that all my expectations will be fulfilled.
- I decree and declare that the blessing of the Lord will make me rich and add no sorrow. **~Proverbs 10:22**
- I decree and declare that the Lord will hasten to perform His word concerning my purpose and destiny. **~Jeremiah 1:12**
- I decree and declare that promotion and progress shall locate me.
- I decree and declare that I will be the head and not the tail and I am above and not beneath. **~Deuteronomy 28:13**
- I decree and declare that the goodness and mercy shall follow me all the days of my life. **~Psalm 23:6**
- I decree and declare God is not only giving me favor with Him, but with man. **~Proverbs 3:4**
- I decree and declare the Lord is opening doors for me that no man can shut. **~Revelation 3:8**
- I decree and declare the spirits of stagnation and procrastination is released from their diabolical assignments.

- I decree and declare that I am in my correcting timing and season to receive the blessings of the Lord. **~Ecclesiastes 3:1**
- I decree and declare that every barrier and limitation over my life is broken and will no longer prevent me from progressing.
- I decree and declare that God is enlarging my territory. **~Exodus 34:24**
- I decree and declare the enemy can no longer hold onto my blessing and it will be released to me seven-fold. **~Proverbs 6:31**
- I decree and declare because I'm walking upright before God, no good thing will He withhold from me. **~Psalm 84:11**
- I decree and declare God is dethroning all demonic agents sitting on my promotion.
- I decree and declare that I will prosper and have a good future because I'm trusting the plans God has for me. **~Jeremiah 29:11**
- I decree and declare that promotion comes from God and He is the one that sets up and puts down according to His will. **~Psalm 75:6-7**
- I decree and declare that as I humble myself, God is strategically orchestrating my divine promotion. **~1 Peter 5:6**

- I decree and declare that the lifter of my head is seating me with princes. ~**Psalm 113:8**
- I decree and declare my gift is making room for me and is bringing me before great men. ~**Proverbs 18:16**

I seal these declarations in the name of Jesus!
Amen

DECLARATIONS FOR BUSINESS

The bible declares that God give us the power to get wealth (Deuteronomy 8:18). This shows God's approval for you to own your business or become an entrepreneur. It is imperative that you know what your purpose and calling is so you can use it both in the kingdom of God and in the marketplace. He desires to have citizens of the kingdom of God to rule and reign in many areas so the agenda of heaven can be carried out. Once you are aware of your purpose, God can download witty ideas and inventions into your spirit. Everyone has a mandate to work the vision God gave to them as well as preparing oneself for the takeover and establishment. Preparation for the takeover includes but is not limited to obtaining certificates and degrees. There are many who speak about faith, which I commend, but faith must be combined with action in order to experience success.

In many instances we have allowed fear to convince us that what God has spoken cannot be manifested because we are looking at our connections, resources, bank accounts or the fact that we feel as though someone is already doing it. If God gave it to you, the business will manifest, and you will not be made ashamed. For example, do you know how many hair or nail salons are throughout the world? This does not deter persons with these gifts and talents from entering the market. Know that there can be the same type of business, but the strategies will always be different based on your gifts, talents and the instructions God gave to you. Also, there may be an invention that no one has ever seen before. Remember, keep your spirit open to what God wants to do in your life.

- I decree and declare God is destroying every barrier and hindrance to my success and breakthrough in business.
- I decree and declare the eyes of my spirit function with correct accuracy to see witty ideas, inventions and instructions from God. ~**Ephesians 1:18**
- I decree and declare God is sending resources from the north, south, east and west to aid in the building up of my business.
- I decree and declare the wind of God is blowing afresh on my business daily.
- I decree and declare God did not give me the spirit of fear so I will move boldly with my business. ~**2 Timothy 1:7**

- I decree and declare that everything I put my hands to do will prosper. **~Deuteronomy 30:9**
- I decree and declare the blood of Jesus covers and protects my business.
- I decree and declare the favor of God is going before every business meeting and everything associated with my business.
- I decree and declare open doors and new markets for my company's goods and services. **~Isaiah 22:22**
- I decree and declare that my business will be unique and stand out from the rest.
- I decree and declare the success of my business is not by might nor by power, but by the spirit of the Lord. **~Zechariah 4:6**
- I decree and declare God is sending clients with the necessary funds to patronize the business.
- I decree and declare that my business will owe no financial institution because we are the lenders and not the borrowers. **~Deuteronomy 28:12**
- I decree and declare God is sending ethical and trustworthy employees to be a part of the business.
- I decree and declare that all employees will operate in unity and oneness. **~Ephesians 4:3**

- I decree and declare I will submit to the will of God for my business every day.
- I decree and declare my gifts and products are making room for the business. **~Proverbs 18:16**
- I decree and declare that every cycle of failure launched against my business is broken.
- I decree and declare that nothing is impossible with God for my business. **~Luke 1:37**
- I decree and declare that my company will be a billion-dollar company.

I seal these declarations in the name of Jesus!
Amen

DECLARATIONS FOR FINANCES

God's desire is for us to live an abundant and prosperous life (John 10:10). We can find confidence in knowing that God will supply all our needs according to his riches in glory. This means that we should not look to mankind as our source but to God himself. However, we are mandated by God to bring our tithes and offering into the storehouses and He will open the floodgates of Heaven for us (Malachi 3:10).

God is aware of your situation and knows that in order for manifestation to happen in your life it has to come by way of the natural realm. God will continue to be Jehovah Jireh once you call on him. Remember that you will never be put to shame if you are abiding by the word and principles of God. Always seek to be a blessing to others because these are seeds that you are sowing and when the harvest is ripe you will reap what you sow. The word of God declares that your giving can reap pressed down, shaken together, and running over blessings (Luke 6:38). Trust that God is working out every financial situation according to His will and plan for your life.

- I decree and declare I will pay ten percent of everything earned according to the word of God. **~Genesis 28:22**
- I decree and declare that God is rebuking the devour for my sake. **~Malachi 3:11**
- I decree and declare the windows of heaven has opened for me and I will not have enough room to contain it. **~Malachi 3:10**
- I decree and declare the abundance of financial blessings will allow me to be a blessing to others.
- I decree and declare God is always providing seed to the sower. **~2 Corinthians 9:10**
- I decree and declare that I am a money magnet.
- I decree and declare that I will be the first billionaire in my family.
- By the power of the Holy Ghost, I destroy all generational curses assigned to keep me in lack.
- I decree and declare the fire of God is destroying anything buried under the ground to bring poverty in my life.
- I decree and declare God is multiplying my money and talents like the wise men

in the parable of the talents. ~**Matthew 25:29**

- I decree and declare that I will be a good steward over my finances and will not squander my money unnecessarily. ~**Proverbs 13:18**
- I decree and declare because the Lord is my shepherd I shall not lack or want anything. ~**Psalm 23:1**
- I decree and declare every mark of poverty is removed from my life.
- I decree and declare every trap of poverty is disgraced by the power of God.
- I decree and declare God is contending with those that contend with me for my financial freedom. ~**Isaiah 49:25**
- I decree and declare any demonic transaction pertaining to my finances that has taken place in the spiritual realm and was designed to keep me in a cycle, may the blood of Jesus be against you.

I seal these declarations in the name of Jesus!
Amen

DECLARATIONS AGAINST THE SPIRIT OF DELAY

Waiting on God is never easy, but when we can rest in Him the wait becomes easier. Isaiah 40:31 declares the Lord shall renew the strength of those that wait on Him and during the waiting period they won't be weary or faint. Always remember that if God is making you wait it is because He does not want you to mishandle the blessing. If the blessing comes before the predestined time, what should be a blessing to you could now be viewed or operate as a curse due to your inability to carry it.

Additionally, there are times when the enemy will set up roadblocks, hindrances or invisible barriers to prevent you from reaching your destiny at the appointed time. This is one way of identifying whether you are waiting on God's perfect timing or whether a spirit of delay is in operation. Always be prayerful and sober minded so you can wage war against this spirit.

- I decree and declare every spirit of delay is destroyed by the fire of God.

- I decree and declare God is providing clarity on every situation that is causing confusion. **~1 Corinthians 14:33**
- I decree and declare every spirit of repeated cycles are destroyed by fire.
- I decree and declare that I will submit myself to God and resist the temptation of getting caught up in any situation that will cause a delay in my life. **~James 4:7**
- I decree and declare every generational curse is broken that would release a spirit of delay in my life.
- I decree and declare that any covenant and curse sent to delay my progress will fall and die.
- I decree and declare I have favor with God and with man. **~Proverbs 3:4**
- I decree and declare every spirit of sluggishness and backwardness in my life receive the fire of God now and be destroyed.
- I decree and declare the breakers anointing is destroying all curses operating in my family lineage. **~Micah 2:13**
- I decree and declare the anointing of an overcomer will rest upon me to pursue, overtake and recover all. **~1 Samuel 30:18**

- I decree and declare all spiritual cages blocking my progress and breakthrough be destroyed by the fire of God.
- I decree and declare every demonic alter that has my name and property on it be destroyed by the wind of God.
  ~Deuteronomy 7:5
- I decree and declare every cycle of failure, disappointment, setback and frustration be destroyed by the blood of Jesus.
- I decree and declare any power trying to keep me in one spot shall fall and die.
- I decree and declare every curse set up against my destiny will shatter to pieces.
  ~Exodus 34:13
- I decree and declare that every curse is being turned into blessings.
  ~Deuteronomy 23:5
- I decree and declare the lifter of my head is raising me above every spirit that is trying to bring me down. **~Psalm 3:3**
- I decree and declare everything sent to frustrate me from completing my assignment I have crushed and is under my feet. **~Psalm 18:38**

I seal these declarations in the name of Jesus!
Amen

DECLARATIONS AGAINST MIND BATTLES

One of the areas that many are being fought in by the enemy is the mind. Do not be naive in not knowing the capacity of how powerful the mind is. The mind is where our thoughts reside, and this is one of the places where God speaks to us. God is a great father and wants to keep us abreast of what He is thinking and doing, which is why He downloads His thoughts in our minds. Now, can you understand why you may be experiencing mind battles. The reason why the enemy uses mind battles against an individual is to bring about a spirit of confusion. When an individual is confused, they will have difficulties making decisions, they will begin to second guess themselves and this can cause a disruption in their everyday life. Second guessing oneself can make you feel as though something is wrong with you and there is the potential for persons view you as unstable. This won't be beneficial to your reputation as the enemy's plan is to always discredit the sanity of individuals.

If the mind is under attack and you do not use the word of God as a defense, it can lead to you questioning your faith level in God. If you begin to waiver in your faith, there is a strong possibility that you will move out of alignment and position, thus forfeiting or even delaying the promises of God. Truth is, wherever the mind goes, so will the rest of the body. This is why the bible declares in Isaiah 26:3 that God will keep those in perfect peace whose mind is stayed on Him. There's a popular saying, "the mind is a terrible thing to waste." I admonish you to renew and wash your mind with the word of God daily to prevent and combat mind battles.

- I decree and declare that I will humble myself and submit myself under the Lordship of Jesus Christ and He will exalt me in due season. ~**1 Peter 5:6**
- I decree and declare the fire of God is destroying every demonic frequency trying to come against my mind.
- I decree and declare I will resist the devil, so he must flee from my presence. ~**James 4:7**
- I decree and declare this peace I have the world didn't give it to me so they can't take it away. ~**John 14:27**
- I decree and declare every demonic prophetic word spoken over my life to cause me to walk contrary to the will of God for my life is broken.

- I decree and declare that I have the mind of Christ, therefore my mind cannot be penetrated by darkness. **~1 Corinthians 2:16**
- I decree and declare the God of Elijah will answer by fire all spirits of Alzheimer's, forgetfulness, dementia, and mind battles today.
- I decree and declare the wrath of God will visit every satanic worker trying to bring destruction to my mind.
- I decree and declare I am fighting the good fight of faith and because of it, my inner man is becoming stronger. **~1 Timothy 6:12**
- I decree and declare that I will not breakdown, but I will experience breakthrough.
- I decree and declare that when the enemy is coming against my mind like a flood, the spirit of the Lord is lifting a standard against him. **~Isaiah 59:19**
- I decree and declare that any time the enemy comes against me one way, he will scatter and flee several different ways. **~Deuteronomy 28:7**
- I decree and declare God is removing everything that is causing grief, stress and sorrow in my life.

- I decree and declare the spirit of fear and anxiety is dismantled and stripped from its power. **~2 Timothy 1:7; Philippians 4:6-7**
- I decree and declare the blood of Jesus blocks all mind manipulation through astral projections and monitoring spirits.
- Lord, I declare that as you guide my path and footsteps that you are causing my enemies to be at peace with me. **~Proverbs 16:7**
- I decree and declare I am taking every thought captive that exalts itself against the knowledge of Jesus Christ. **~2 Corinthians 10:5**
- I decree and declare a sound mind and peace of mind is my portion. **~2 Timothy 1:7**
- I decree and declare that I will not be my own enemy.
- Lord, I know that no matter what I may be facing, you are near to me because I call on you. **~Psalm 145:18**

I seal these declarations in the name of Jesus!
Amen

DECLARATIONS AGAINST THE SPIRIT OF REJECTION

One of the things individuals are always looking for is acceptance from others. Not achieving acceptance from others can cause many to develop feelings of rejection or inadequacy. It is important that persons who may have experienced rejection in childhood ensure the spirit of rejection is dealt with, so it doesn't affect their adult life. Unresolved issues with the spirit of rejection can cause many relational problems and affect your life without you even knowing it. For example, if you were rejected throughout your childhood, it can make you overly sensitive and cause you to sabotage any new impending relationship because you feel the person may reject you. Psychologically, this is how you would enter in a defensive mode to protect your feelings or yourself from being hurt by someone else. If you continuously do this, you can find yourself experiencing other feelings such as loneliness and the possibility of depression if you are unable to handle rejection.

Rejection is simply the act of not accepting something or someone we do not want or cannot afford. Do you realize you reject things every day? For example, if you choose to carry lunch to work daily and not purchase fast food, you are rejecting all possible fast food options even if you are doing it for the purpose of saving money. Do you think that if you choose not to buy fast food it will hinder the establishment from earning money? No, this is one of the ways you will need to view your life if you are going to be successful in not allowing the spirit of rejection to hinder your progress.

The destiny that God has assigned for you will require you to experience rejection at times. Unfortunately, no matter how painful it is, this is a part of life. For many of you, there are persons who are unable to go where God is taking you so the separation will come. Sometimes God will allow the rejection because you are too comfortable, and He needs you to move so that the work He desires to do in you can be done. Have you ever been in a situation that God told you to leave and you refused to do it in his timing? What happened? Did everything that could go wrong start to go wrong? You must understand that delayed obedience is still disobedience. God has the master blueprint for your life and sometimes he orchestrates rejection in order to redirect you. No one will ever understand why God does what He does because his ways and thoughts are far above our finite minds. The bible states that no servant is greater than his master and if Jesus experienced rejection this means that you will not be exempted.

- I decree and declare when my father and mother abandon me, the Lord will hold me close. **~Psalm 27:10**
- I decree and declare the good work God has started in me He will see it to completion. **~Philippians 1:6**
- Lord, help me to truly forgive those who would have rejected me.
- I decree and declare I am fearful and wonderfully made and therefore I am perfect in God's eyes. **~Psalm 139:14**
- I decree and declare the love of God will flow abundantly in my life. **~1 Timothy 1:14**
- I decree and declare you came to set me free from every demonic spirit that is keeping me bound and stagnated. **~John 8:36**
- I decree and declare that if God be for me, who can be against me. **~Romans 8:31**
- I decree and declare the LORD will not reject me or forsake His inheritance. **~Psalm 94:14**

- Lord, I dismantle every spirit of rejection and abandonment from operating in my life.
- Lord, I know that all things are working together for my good because I love you. **~Romans 8:28**
- I decree and declare all voices of the enemy that would want to say that I am unworthy is silenced.
- I decree and declare the will of God will be done in my life and I will not be put to shame because I believe in God. **~Romans 10:11**
- I decree and declare every demonic mark causing rejection be destroyed by the blood of Jesus.
- Lord, I thank you for your compassion and mercy displayed towards me because I fear you. **~Psalm 103:13**
- I decree and declare that the favor of God is resting upon my life and no good thing will He withhold from me. **~Psalm 84:11**
- Lord, I come against all spirits of rejection that came by way of generational curses with the blood of Jesus.
- I decree and declare that weeping may endure for a night, but my joy is coming int the morning. **~Psalm 30:5**

- I decree and declare the truth will prevail in my life against every enemy. **~Isaiah 42:13**
- Lord, I come against every spirit of jealousy and hatred that would cause people to reject me.
- I decree and declare that I may not be man's choice, but I am God's choice.

I seal these declarations in the name of Jesus!
Amen

DECLARATIONS FOR PROTECTION

Throughout the bible we notice that God will always send His angels or provide instructions via the Holy Spirit to protect people from danger. If God is the same yesterday, today and forever more, all we have to do is call unto Him and He will come to our rescue because of His love for us. There are times that we may have gotten ourselves into situations due to disobedience, but God's grace and mercy keeps us. However, we must not take his grace and mercy for granted when He rescues us out of various situations. The bible declares to us that demons tremble at the very name of Jesus, so when you don't know what to say all you simply have to do is call on the name of Jesus.

Remember that God is always protecting us from seen and unseen dangers on a daily basis as there is an enemy that is constantly warring for our soul and seeking whom he can devour. Stay in position and in a posture having clean hands and a pure heart if you desire for God's word to protect you. Using the sword of the Lord (bible) during prayer, penetrates the kingdom of darkness and causes God to respond to His word, because He is a man that cannot lie, and His word will not return unto Him void. Make a conscientious effort to clad yourself in the full armor of God daily so you can withstand the attacks of the enemy.

- I decree and declare the blood of Jesus covers me from the crown of my head to the soles of my feet.
- I decree and declare that I dwell in the secret place of the of the most High and abide under the shadow of the Almighty. **~Psalm 91:1**
- I decree and declare no weapon formed against me shall prosper. **~Isaiah 54:17**
- I decree and declare the Lord is giving his angels charge over me to keep me in all my ways. **~Psalm 91:11**
- I decree and declare that God is a pillar of cloud by day and a pillar of fire by night for me and my family. **~Exodus 13:21**
- Lord, continue to make every crooked path straight on my behalf. **~Isaiah 45:2**
- I decree and declare the God of Elijah is answering every one of my enemies by fire.
- I decree and declare God is breaking into pieces the gates of brass over my life. **~Isaiah 45:2**

- I decree and declare that as I put on the whole armor of God, that I can stand against the wiles of the devil. **~Ephesians 6:11**
- Lord, send a spirit of ambushment into the enemy's camp as you did with King Jehoshaphat so I can pursue, overtake and recover all. **~2 Chronicles 20:22**
- I decree and declare Jehovah Gibbor is arising and every one of my enemies are being scattered. **~Psalm 68:1**
- I decree and declare goodness and mercy shall follow me all the days of my life. **~Psalm 23:6**
- Lord, let the King of Glory, the Lord strong and mighty fight my battles. **~Psalm 24:8**
- I decree and declare God is increasing my level of discernment so I can pick up demonic activity in the realm of the spirit before it launches so I won't be deceived.
- I decree and declare there is no need for me to fight my battles because vengeance is the Lord. **~Romans 12:19**
- I cancel all demonic assignments and generational curses that rise against me and my family.
- Lord, blind the eyes and deafen the ears of all monitoring spirits.

- Lord, I always keep at the forefront of my mind that I'm not wrestling against flesh and blood, but against principalities, powers, rulers of the darkness and spiritual wickedness in high places. **~Ephesians 6:12**
- I decree and declare, the Egyptians that I see today I will see them no more. **~Exodus 14:13**
- I cancel every spirit of Jezebel, Ahab, Pharaoh, Haman and Judas that would try to stop me from fulfilling my God ordained purpose and prevent me from living an abundant life.

I seal these declarations in the name of Jesus!

Amen

FASTING

Fasting is abstaining from food for a period of time. There will be times that you incur intense warfare in your life and declarations, or prayers alone will not be sufficient. Incorporating declarations with a fast will destroy yokes and break the bands of wickedness off your life (Isaiah 58:6). Matthew 17:21 declares there are some strongholds that requires fasting if you are going to be set free from bondage. Strongholds can be viewed as a fortified area in which the enemy fights us in. If there is an area in your life that you have been praying about for many years and haven't gotten a breakthrough, there is a possibility that it is because a stronghold is present.

God declares that He came to set the captives free and this is an assurance that you have power whenever you encounter a stronghold. Always remember that we don't wrestle against flesh and blood, so your battle is not with people, but evil spirits that are in operation behind the individual. Always ask God to reveal to you the spirits that are in operation so you can wage war against them. Once you have been released from what was holding you down and locking up your destiny, the increase will occur. This is because now the areas in your life that you were struggling in will be accelerated and there will be no blockage.

There are different types of fasts that can be done. However, it is imperative to be in a state of true repentance and humility before embarking upon any fast if God is going to hear your prayers/declarations. Fasting is not designed to change or manipulate God, but to change you and bring deliverance. Those who partake in fasting will experience a deeper level of intimacy with God because of the new revelations that will be downloaded.

This is one of the ways God expresses His desires for us and gives us insight into His perspective. It is vital that you treat fasting as a sacred time and not boast about this time (Matthew 6:16-18). During your time of fasting, be careful not to get into arguments, use words of profanity or engage in sinful acts to prevent the fast from being ineffective or even worse, reinforcing the very stronghold that you were believing God to break during the fast.

Benefits of Prayer & Fasting

When combined with prayer and a sincere passion for God, fasting can have a powerful influence on the effectiveness of our prayer life as well as our spiritual relationship with the Lord. Prayer with fasting is an act that we will see throughout the bible by various individuals for many different reasons. It is crucial that every believer practice this on a regular and frequent basis to help them while on their spiritual journey with God. It is also vital that when embarking upon prayer and fasting that you come before God humbly and with a heart of repentance.

Fasting is more that abstaining from food, but it is much more than that. The intent is to withdraw our attention from earthly and physical things and people so we can focus more on spiritual things and God. While fasting, it is important that you spend time eating the word of God which aids in increasing your spiritual muscles. This causes us to develop discipline in order to humble and submit our flesh to God. Doing this helps us to ensure that our fleshly desires will not get the best of us or have the ability to manipulate us because we have the Holy Spirit dwelling in us.

Prayer and fasting can be seen as intense worship and devotion towards God. This can be done individually or as a group. This is the time to lean on God and draw on His strength. As you draw closer to God, your appetite will increase for the things of God. A war is constantly going on in the spiritual realm concerning your soul and this is why we must learn to surrender to God and take up our cross daily. We must learn to be led by the spirit in our thoughts, decisions and lifestyle, rather than the nature of our flesh.

Prayer and fasting also increases our faith in God because we are spending more time in God's word. The bible declares in Romans 10:17 "faith cometh by hearing and hearing by the word of God." The more we hear it, the more our spirit will digest it. This allows us to combat any carnal feelings or influences because we are building our spiritual muscles. As we detox our spirits of fleshly or carnal desires, our confidences in God grows on a much deeper level. Hence, this is why prayer and fasting is important and beneficial to our daily walk.

Discerning God's Voice

Spending time in prayer and fasting allows our spirit man to be heightened, thus causing us to hear the voice of God more clearly. This is also the time to ask God to train you in hearing the sound of His voice. Because we live in a natural world, we will always be faced with chaos and things of this world. However, even in the midst of the chaos, you can learn to discern God's voice because you would have spent time in His presence. I admonish you to always pray and fast before making major decisions such as getting married, investing in a home and much more to prevent setbacks within your life.

Renewed Desire for God

Truth is, the chaos of daily life can cause us to stray away from God as we are not intentional about spending quality time with him. For many, the fire has gone out or is barely burning and we have lost our first love. Sacrifice must be on the altar for a renewed desire of God to take place. Only, when we enter the presence of God is when we realize how much we have missed the mark in our relationship with him. The state of our relationship must always be at the forefront of our minds. It's through prayer and fasting that we learn how vital it is in order to live the abundant life God promised us. The bible declares in John 4:14 that "whosoever drinketh of the water that I shall give him shall never thirst; but the water that I shall give him shall be in him a well of water springing up into everlasting life." This scripture indicates to me that only God can quench and fill any desire we truly have. The good news is, God is always waiting with open arms to rekindle the love affair and He only desires a closer relationship with you.

Fasting gives us power to break demonic strongholds

The bible declares in Mark 9:29 "this kind can come forth by nothing, but by prayer and fasting." This scripture indicates to me that there are times when reinforcement is needed due to the stronghold. A stronghold is anything that acts as a stubborn hinderance to your breakthrough. Isaiah 58:6 declares "is not this the fast that I have chosen? To loose the bands of wickedness, to undo the heavy burdens, and to let the oppressed go free, and that ye break every yoke?" God is not a God that He should lie and as we examine this scripture, we will recognize that this is a way for us to break free from generational curses and anything that has you oppressed.

As you engage in the combination of prayer and fasting, expect strongholds to be broken. Always seek God for the length of intense prayer and fasting (warfare) needed to break a specific stronghold in your life. Daniel 10:12-13 says, "Then said he unto me, Fear not, Daniel: for from the first day that thou didst set thine heart to understand, and to chasten thyself before thy God, thy words were heard, and I am come for thy words. But the prince of the kingdom of Persia withstood me one and twenty days: but, lo, Michael, one of the chief princes, came to help me; and I remained there with the kings of Persia." For Daniel, his breakthrough took twenty-one days despite God hearing his prayer from the very first day. This means you have to persevere in prayer and do not retreat even if it seems or look as though God didn't hear your prayer. Always make it a point to express to God what you desire to achieve or accomplish by the end of the fast.

Fasting invokes protection and favor of God

There are times when fasting invokes the favor and protection of God. This is the time when you have to cry out to God for grace and mercy. The bible declares in Esther 4:16 "Go, gather together all the Jews that are present in

Shushan, and fast ye for me, and neither eat nor drink three days, night or day: I also and my maidens will fast likewise; and so will I go in unto the king, which *is* not according to the law: and if I perish, I perish". This was a time when the Jews were facing persecution because of a decree sent out due to evil intentions from Haman. However, a three-day fast was called and God granted Esther favor with the King, thus saving her people (Jews). We must always remember that the heart of kings are in the hand of God and He can turn it whichever way He chooses.

In the New Testament, Prophetess Anna is praised in the book of Luke for being a devoted servant to God and His temple. Because she regularly fasted and prayed, she was able to hear the voice of God speak clearly to her the day that Baby Jesus was brought into the temple to be dedicated. She knew He was the Christ and told everyone who would listen about His arrival. When we detox our spirit and become consumed with a desire and praise for God, we become sensitive to His voice. Like Anna, when God speaks to us in the midst of chaos, we'll be able to discern His voice and know what He wants us to do because we have trained our ears to hear Him through fasting, prayer, study and praise.

Three Types of Fast

Esther Fast

The Esther fast which is sometimes called a dry fast because you will not eat or drink anything. This fast usually lasts for three (3) days (Esther 4:16). This was a time when Esther and the Jews in the land was fasting for favor when she approached the king without invitation and for the protection of the Jewish people who she was a part of.

The Daniel Fast

During the Daniel fast you will not eat any meat, bread or anything sweet. When on this fast you will only drink water and juice and eat fruits and vegetables. This fast is usually done for twenty-one days (Daniel 10:3).

40 Days and 40 Nights

This fast was done by Jesus when He was led to the wilderness by the Holy Spirit to be tempted by the devil (Matthew 4:1). During this time Jesus only drank water. This fast is for those who are mature in their faith and fasting.

I admonish you to allow the Holy Spirit to lead you when to fast, the type of fast that He desires from you as well as the amount of days required for fasting. There are times when these fast are done and modification is used. Please use wisdom and consult with a medical physician before attempting a fast.

THE POWER OF WORDS JOURNAL

In many instances we are unaware of the power of our words and whether they make a positive or negative impact. If we speak negatively, we cancel the promises of God for our lives and if we speak positively, we come into agreement with the promises of God. For the next 5 days, journal the words that you have been speaking. By doing this, you will become more aware of what you speak daily.

THE POWER OF WORDS DAY 1

_____

_____

_____

_____

_____

_____

_____

_____

_____

_____

_____

_____

_____

_____

_____

_____

_____

_____
_____
_____
_____
_____
_____
_____
_____
_____
_____
_____
_____
_____
_____
_____
_____
_____
_____
_____

_____

_____

_____

_____

_____

_____

_____

_____

_____

_____

_____

_____

_____

_____

_____

_____

THE POWER OF WORDS DAY 2

_____

_____

_____

_____

_____

_____

_____

_____

_____

_____

_____

_____

_____

_____

_____

I Declare War: Spiritual Warfare Declarations

_____

_____

_____

_____

_____

_____

_____

_____

_____

_____

_____

_____

_____

_____

_____

_____

_____

_____

_____

_____

_____

_____

_____

_____

_____

_____

_____

_____

_____

_____

_____

_____

_____

_____

_____

_____

_____

_____

THE POWER OF WORDS DAY 3

_____

_____

_____

_____

_____

_____

_____

_____

_____

_____

_____

_____

_____

_____

_____

_____

_____

_____

_____

_____

_____

_____

_____

_____

_____

_____

_____

_____

_____

_____

_____

_____

_____

_____

_____

_____

_____

_____

_____

_____

_____

_____

_____

_____

_____

_____

_____

_____

_____

_____

_____

_____

_____

_____

THE POWER OF WORDS DAY 4

_____

_____

_____

_____

_____

_____

_____

_____

_____

_____

_____

_____

_____

_____

_____

_____

_____

_____

_____

_____

_____

_____

_____

_____

_____

_____

_____

_____

_____

_____

_____

_____

_____

_____

_____

_____

_____

_____

_____

_____

_____

_____

_____

_____

_____

_____

_____

_____

_____

THE POWER OF WORDS DAY 5

_____

_____

_____

_____

_____

_____

_____

_____

_____

_____

_____

_____

_____

_____

_____

_____

_____

_____
_____
_____
_____
_____
_____
_____
_____
_____
_____
_____
_____
_____
_____
_____
_____

_____

_____

_____

_____

_____

_____

_____

_____

_____

_____

_____

_____

_____

_____

_____

_____

_____

_____

_____

REFLECTION

Always remember that you have the power to change your situation based on what you decree. The bible declares out of the heart flows the issues of life. Many of you have experienced various trials and tribulations in life that has caused your speech to change negatively and now there is a distorted view concerning your destiny. Unfortunately, some no longer believe they can have what God says they can have. Truth is, many of you have the faith to believe more for others than for yourselves. What do you think would happen if you used that same faith level for yourself? Are you afraid that what you are believing God for can actually manifest? The ultimate goal is to ensure you change your declaration which will lead to you changing your behavior to bring you back into alignment.

Use the next set of questions as a guide to reflect on your yesterday, today, and tomorrow. Think about the questions and your life before writing. Let the questions challenge you to go deep and pull out things you may have hidden or have pushed aside that needs to be brought out to the forefront.

What would happen if you looked at your story differently?

_____

_____

_____

_____

_____

_____

_____

_____

_____

_____

_____

_____

_____

_____

_____

What is hindering your future? What do you think can happen if you allowed the past to stay in the past?

_____

_____

_____

_____

_____

_____

_____

_____

_____

_____

_____

_____

_____

_____

What if you decided to put the future in the present or now?

_____

_____

_____

_____

_____

_____

_____

_____

_____

_____

_____

_____

_____

_____

What do you think would happen if you made a conscientious effort to change your outlook?

_____

_____

_____

_____

_____

_____

_____

_____

_____

_____

_____

_____

_____

_____

_____

_____

Assess where you are in your life now and where you want to be in the future. Then, develop ten (10) personal declarations that you can use to declare to shift you to where you want to be.

_____

_____

_____

_____

_____

_____

_____

_____

_____

_____

_____

_____

_____

_____

ABOUT THE AUTHOR

Dr. Tavara Johnson is an event host, speaker, author and mentor who is dedicated and passionate about the pursuit of purpose.

Dr. Johnson is the visionary of Jewels and Gems and Distinctive Women of Worth (DWOW) which were founded to assist women in finding their God-given purpose and experience healing in their 'inner me'. She has hosted numerous empowerment events yearly via Jewels and Gems and monthly via DWOW to provide women in attendance the opportunity to break free from bondage and experience freedom at every level.

She believes women who are healed and whole have the opportunity to live an abundant life and reach the destiny God has designed for them. Her training in the area of Christian Counselling provides her with the knowledge and skills to help women examine their current state, identify obstacles or challenges and choose a plan of action to propel them to their next level. She knows that she has been called to serve, inspire and empower other women on their personal journey to greatness.

Dr. Johnson has obtained her Doctorate Degree in the Ministry of Christian Counselling from Jacksonville Theological Seminary, Master's Degree in Business Administration with emphasis in Human Resources Management from Keller Graduate School of Management and a Bachelor of Science Degree in Technical Management from DeVry University. She is a Human Resources professional and has been working in this field for the past twelve years.

Her journey to impact women and fulfill her life's purpose has led her to grace the cover of K.I.SH. Magazine and to be featured in K.I.S.H Magazine, Beautilicious Beauty Magazine and

UpWords Magazine (India). In addition, she has appeared as a guest on The Dreamer in You TV Show, Blossoms of my Life Radio Show, God's Gems Radio Show, Kishma George Radio Show and The Good Deeds Radio Show. She is also the recipient of The Beautillcious 'Be Your Own Kind of Beautiful Award' (2019) and the K.I.S.H Magazine Woman of the Year Honoree (2019).

She has recently launched the Woman II Woman (WIIW) Mentorship Program for single women to help them embrace the new. WIIW will help singles harness their next level and move them into alignment. Additionally, she is the author of the singles devotional 'The Weight of the Wait', co-author of Dreamer on the Rise, and her life's mantra is "people make time for whatever is important to them".

To contact Tavara Johnson visit:

www.tavarajohnson.com

ACKNOWLEDGEMENTS

Firstly, I would like to give God thanks for giving me this vision and trusting me as a vessel to help deliver His people.

To my stepfather and mother, Derek & Valderine Williams, thank you for your constant support and words of encouragement.

To my father and stepmother, Brister & Faye Johnson, thank you for your love and support.

To my siblings, Leslie, Lennette, Amanda, and Bria, thank you for support, love and always believing in me.

To my nieces Mischael, Melinda and Giada, thank you for your hugs and always believing in me.

To Debbie, thank you for your love and always supporting my vision.

To my Apostles, Tony & Anne Grant thank you for your prayers, love and support always.

To Kenisha Missick, thank you for your support and encouraging words always.

A special thank you to Brittany Williams and Prophetess Illiana Joseph for your prayers and encouragement and I thank God for you both.

A special thank you to Jekalyn Carr for your support and your words of encouragement.

To Tamika Woodard (Publisher), thank you for believing in me and trusting the vision God gave to me.

A special thank you to Dr. Kishma George for your prayers, support, always believing in me and encouraging me to know that dreams do come true.

Lastly, I would like to thank Preston Knowles Photography, Huge Impact Marketing, Patrice Forbes and everyone who encouraged, supported and prayed for Jewels & Gems and Distinctive Women of Worth, over the years. I'm forever grateful.

www.ingramcontent.com/pod-product-compliance
Lightning Source LLC
Chambersburg PA
CBHW071100090426
42737CB00013B/2407